THE ACTRESS WITHIN

REFLECTIONS ON GRIEF

BY

JEAN HILL

Copyright © 2019. Jean Hill. All rights reserved

ISBN: 978-0-244-85285-6

Printed and Distributed by Lulu.com

First Published: January 2020

First Edition

Other Work by **Jean Hill**

The Sting In The Tale
Poems and Short Stories

The Barb In The Rhyme

The Lyric In The Lines

The Thorn In The Verse

Poems to make you laugh and cry

and

Let's Smile Again
A Humorous Account of Family Life in the Seventies

Available from: Lulu.com
Amazon &
Other Bookstores

Hold Tight to Each Precious Memory

In Memory Of My Husband

Christopher Robin Hill
'Robin'

11.8.1937 – 5.9.2019

'A Lovely Man'

When We Walk Alone

INTRODUCTION

The Actress Within is a book I could never in my wildest dreams have thought I would ever write. But there is a compelling need. A need deep within myself and those who suffer the pain of bereavement to share. To help, to understand, to bring comfort, to give hope when we're facing the bleakest time of our lives.

Only those who have loved and grieved deeply will realise the necessity of this book. Only those who have lost a loved one will fully comprehend the experiences shared. Bereavement is the least understood emotion.

My aim in writing this book is to say that you're not alone and your feelings are normal. There are millions of bereaved souls out there struggling to come to terms with their loss. I am one of them. Outwardly I carry on with life – I'm a brilliant actress! My face may be arranged in the semblance of a smile but, like you, my heart is breaking.

Perhaps we will forge another life for ourselves, a different life – not one we would wish for, but one we will face together. At some time I hope peace and love will make your life worth living again.

The Greater the Love

The Deeper the Grief

ACKNOWLEDGEMENTS

Deborah … for the front cover arrangement and for being so hugely supportive in the production of this sixth book.

Sharon … for suggesting the title of this book.

Samantha, Benjamin and **Jamie** … for just being.

The talented members of Wokingham Library Poetry Group for support and inspiration.

All my wonderful friends and extended family without whom I could never have coped

THANK YOU ALL

The Legacy of a Wonderful Husband,

Father and Grandfather

Is the Loving Family who Grieve

THE PAIN OF GRIEF

If you look along the shelves of any pharmacy you will find remedies for everything from dandruff to athletes foot, from headaches to haemorrhoids. Pain relief for every pain, ache or discomfort imaginable. But there's one vital pain relief remedy you'll never find. Where is the magic potion that will relieve the searing pain of grief?

Grief is never talked about; it's embarrassing and something one is urged to 'get over' as quickly as possible – probably in the time-span judged adequate by those around us. It's frightening in its intensity to those who witness grief – it could happen to them one day – and it probably will!

To grieve deeply one must have loved deeply – you don't experience one without the other. The greater the love – the deeper the grief. This is true.

THE EFFECT OF GRIEF

We all experience grief in different ways. Nothing is right and nothing is wrong. The strongest amongst us become the weakest and most vulnerable in this time of stress. The efficient become the disorientated. Those who were previously considered clever, professional and capable become confused, dithering and seemingly stupid. Such is the power of grief to destroy and shatter into a million painful fragments the grieving and lost soul left behind.

To have lost a parent or grand-parent is indeed very sad, but somehow it seems possible to reach a level of acceptance; this is the way one generation succeeds the other and, for most, after a period of mourning and sorrow, life moves on. To lose a husband/wife or child takes grieving to a whole new level.

My words in this book may not bring you comfort or alleviate your misery. Nothing can do that. My aim is to share and help you understand your emotions as you, by reading this, will share mine.

YOU'RE NORMAL

What you're feeling is normal – no-one else will say this to you. The pit of bleak despair you can't climb out of; the unrelenting misery; the cry that turns into an animal howl when you're overwhelmed by your grief. This is normal. This is grief.

The early weeks and months following a bereavement, when you exist in a fog of disbelief in an unreal and hostile world; the mental anguish of lost memory and disabling panic when even a simple task is insurmountable. This is normal. This is grief.

Although many don't recognise it as such, this really is normal behaviour – you're not going mad – you're grieving.

Three months, a year, three years, and the rawness is still there. Perhaps time will blunt that rawness – I don't know – I haven't reached that point yet.

HAPPINESS

Happiness is elusive
As a moonbeam on the darkest hour
As a fallen leaf on a forest floor
The faded petals of a fragrant flower

Happiness is fleeting
Like a shadow beyond a door ajar
A glancing sunbeam in a stormy sky
A flash of light from a shooting star

Happiness is make-believe
As melting as an ice-cream cone
With hope spun out like candy-floss
The unanswered ring of a telephone

Happiness is wanton
With taunting dreams beyond our reach
For just one moment ours to clasp
A single pebble on a shingle beach

Happiness is mythical
As high we fly with Icarus wings
To pursue in circles, lost in time
To grasp the song the siren sings

WHAT TO SAY

With the best will in the world people don't know what to say to you. They're embarrassed, they're frightened of saying the wrong thing, they don't want to upset you – or they say nothing.

Here is an example of the best and worst things well intentioned friends have said to me.

Best

"Cry if you want to. I'll just walk quietly by your side".

"I understand things will never be the same but, in your sadness, let me be among the friends you'll turn to".

"It's fine to eat three boxes of jelly babies for lunch and a big bag of marshmallows for dinner. Why not!"

"Ring me when you can't sleep. I'll come round and we'll cry together, talk about him, drink wine and eat chocolate biscuits".

"You must be feeling awful – I can't even begin to imagine how hard it must be without him".

"I'll be there to help when things go wrong. And if your sink blocks up – I know a man with a plunger!"

Grief is Akin to Fear

Worst

"Are you better now".
What! I've just lost a husband not had a dose of flu.

"You're doing so well".
Really! Didn't you hear me howling at three this morning?

"You should eat properly".
Yep! How do I force food over the lump in my throat?

"You must get enough sleep".
Good advice! I'll swallow the whole bottle of sleeping pills tonight – that should do the trick.

"You're such a strong person".
Excuse me! You don't see the panic attacks that reduce me to jelly.

"Do you feel you're getting over it".
No! I'm going to feel bloody awful for the next million years.

If your friends or relative have used these phrases, don't be hard on them. They honestly don't know what to say and it's better than saying nothing. They are really trying to help and don't know how.

And The Truly Unbelievable

"Three months is long enough to mourn".
Gulp! I'm going to mourn forever.

"Draw a line under it".
Err! That's what I do if I eat too many calories on a diet day.

"See everything as a 'new beginning'".
Sorry! I can't see anything – my eyes are filled with tears.

"Cheer Up".
Pardon Me! I've lost a husband – not a hamster.

"So you've joined the band of 'merry' widows".
Whoopee! – I'll throw my knickers in the air and party!

Yes, truly unbelievable, and I'm finding it hard to excuse these crass remarks. In a newly bereaved state we are over-sensitive and it hurts. Perhaps in time I'll think of some suitably glib and sarcastic response but, just for now, even the actress within me can't think of a single thing to say.

FEELINGS

In bereavement we go through stages. One such stage is anger, rage and frustration. A friend actually hit the nail on the head: She asked if I was nervous living and sleeping alone in the house. Funny – I used to be, but since my beloved husband died I don't feel fear of anything tangible. I said I didn't care if a burglar broke in and beat me to death – I'd probably thank him, so deep is my grief. There were gasps from those around me, but she understood. She simply said 'The worst that can happen has happened and nothing can ever be that bad again'. She is right.

Like others immersed in a mire of misery, I want to lash out, to hit, to kick, to punch; but society would frown on a manifestation of that level of grief! Yes, I'd welcome a burglar or mugger – I could beat him to a pulp and release my frenzy of rage!

This little spark of feeling is good – before this, in my zombie state, I felt nothing but a chasm of hollow emptiness.

PHYSICAL PAIN

Dealing (or not dealing) with the physical pain of grief is something I would never have imagined. This is not based on any medical opinion, just my own experience. Physical pain brought about by intense stress caused by grief is real – believe me!

The ache in your stomach, the brick which is somehow lodged in your chest, the permanent lump in your throat that makes it impossible to swallow, hair loss, unexplained lesions in your skin, the dull headache and nausea – all real tangible physical health issues which, in my case, were attributed to the stress of acute grief.

And no, you're not becoming a hypochondriac – this is for real and at this point your best friend is a sympathetic doctor. They've seen it all before. Counselling could be suggested and if you feel this would help – go for it. For me, a stranger spouting text book platitudes didn't appeal. Each to their own. I opted for 'magic pills' – perhaps I'm a coward but I couldn't go on fighting this on my own! I would have gone under totally!

Please speak to your doctor – they really have seen it all before.

MENTAL ANGUISH

No – you're not going mad! All your mental faculties are masked by the intensity of your sorrow. Lack of concentration, total inability to think things through or, indeed, to follow any rational line of thought at all. Unable to keep track of a conversation or speak more than half a dozen words without losing the thread of what you're trying to say. Forget about reading a book or newspaper – the words will blur and won't make any sense. The television is just a jumble of flashing images with no coherence. No – you're not going mad; it's grief.

Trying to tackle a simple task like using the bank cash machine creates a panic attack that leaves you crying and shaking in the middle of HSBC. Stopping the car because, having braved driving, you forget where you're going or how to get there. You don't recognise your own road and panic as you don't know where you are. Asking the same question umpteen times and forgetting the answer. Sitting with friends listening to their chatter when a curtain of blackness envelopes you and oblivion overtakes you. Curled up under the duvet in the foetal position clutching a hot-water-bottle, unable to face the day. No – you're not going mad; it's grief.

When you grip the pen so tightly you can't even write your own name and your hand starts to shake. When you stay up because you can't face the blackness of night and going to bed. When you stay in bed because you can't face the day-light and getting up. When the muscles in your face are so tight and your eyes so swollen with tears that you hardly recognise yourself in the mirror. When the buzzing in your brain deafens you. No – you're not going mad; it's grief.

You are suffering the symptoms of overwhelming grief which, unless they have been in that same situation, no-one will truly understand. Let me say again … You are NOT going mad – it's normal – it's grief!

Again I say, please seek medical help.

LEARN TO LEAN

Support from family and friends is all important at this time of bereavement. I could not have coped without the love and never-ending support of my two wonderful, caring daughters. In this respect I am fortunate. For the first few weeks they took over every aspect of my life and how I lived through that time is a blur, a mystery that I can't recall.

I remember holding my husband's hand as he died and kissing him one last time, but after that my mind is a vacuum. With sadness etched on their faces, my daughters helped me survive the shock and horror surrounding the death of my lovely husband.

Although there will always be a gap in their lives when they think of their Dad, their lives must go on. The grand-children will remember their grandad fondly, the extended family will miss him but, for them, the world will, quite rightly continue to turn. Our world stands still, locked in what was and unable to accept what will be.

JOY LOST

The radio plays its mindless tune
In the lonely silence of an empty room
The futile prattle, the platitudes
Bring no joy to my darkened moods

Where are you, you evade my heart
Bereft of joy, you play no part
In searching quest, so lost, forlorn
As I seek your light in a sleepless dawn

Where are you joy in a vacant chair
As seasons change – no-one to share
The summer rose with beauty kissed
The Autumn's chill nocturnal mist

The beam of moonlight through a windowpane
Falls on the pillow where you have lain
My arms reach out in familiar way
For comfort in the sorrow of my grief-filled day

Are you still there by the willow tree
Is your presence felt in a turquoise sea
In turbulent winds on a mountain peak
I cannot find you – yet still I seek

Are you in the warmth of a fireside hearth
In woodlands green and a sun-lit path
In the twinkling light of a Christmas tree
There is no joy to spend time with me

Joy, you are treasured, a memory past
In happiness, pure, too good to last
Perhaps, one day, you'll relieve my pain
Perhaps, one day, we'll meet again

MOVING ON

'Moving On'. What a trite phrase that is. Moving on to what I can hear you ask. Endless eternity? Moving on when? Three months, three years, ten years? One person actually said to me that three months mourning was quite long enough! Unbelievable! They had no understanding of true grief.

I asked one lady who had been a widow for eighteen years if she had been able to move on. She said 'I have a big house, a large garden and more money than I know what to do with, but I would give it all up just to hear his voice again'. Tears rolled down her cheeks.

There is no 'moving on'. In time the best to hope for is some sort of acceptance of the existence we now find ourselves in. Perhaps the raging rawness will blunt but that's a long way off for the newly bereaved. I don't think there's ever going to be a 'getting over it'. We will always long for the past to be present in our lives again, to hear the words of our loved one, to feel their touch, to hold them in our arms and be held. A sideways step perhaps into some sort of manageable life-style we wouldn't have wished for and don't really want. As one friend so rightly said: 'You've joined the club no-one wants to be a member of – that of bereaved widows'.

'Moving on' – I don't think so! Adjustment to the situation we now find ourselves in and a reluctant acceptance – perhaps – in time. A long time. Just now tears still blind us to the future.

You Gave Me Roses

GRIEF IN SOCIETY

Society does not recognise the true pain of acute grief. It's taboo, frightening, embarrassing. It's beyond the comfort zone and sphere of comprehension of anyone who has not actually suffered it. But we, the bereaved, must not be harsh; our friends are kind people, they mean well and want to help – many just don't know how.

As one wise widow who lost her husband many years ago explained: You never recover. It's comparable to losing a limb, an arm or a leg; you won't ever 'get over it' or 'get better'. We must learn to adapt and adjust to our new circumstances. This is the harsh truth that society often fails to acknowledge.

I am sincerely grateful for all the loving care and practical help given to me by my lovely friends. I can't thank them enough. I hope they never have to suffer the intense pain of grief in order to understand it, but I know at some time in their lives they might. I truly hope I will, by then, be in some sort of fit state to help – I will definitely understand!

UNDERSTANDING

Sometimes it is impossible to bring comfort. I can't think of any words that even come close. In its garbled and stumbling way, this book is written to say that I understand your torment. I share and truly know what you are going through. Your emotions are normal. Perhaps knowing that you are not alone in feeling as you do is a small measure of comfort – I don't know. I can only hope so.

Anyone reading these words will say it is the most miserable and depressing book they have ever read. And they will be right. But they are not grieving!

For the newly bereaved (and the not so newly bereaved) it is the most unhappy and distressing time of our lives. To have lost your greatest love is mind-numbing in its totality. In reading this book you are, in a way, sharing my grief as I am sharing yours. I want to reach out and hold your hand, to still your pain and relieve some of your burden, as I hope time, in some way, will ease mine. I understand – truly I do. I too am drowning in an ocean of tears. I understand. Your feelings are normal, the pain of your grief is normal. The tears you shed are normal. The panic attack in Tesco's is normal, when you hold your head in your hands and howl at three in the morning – it's normal. Believe me, it's OK to feel these emotions, you're not going mad, it's the pain of grief for which there is no cure.

You have to have been there to fully understand the actual physical, mental and emotional anguish of grief. However stiff you think your upper lip is, losing the one person in your life you love the most reduces the strongest to a zombie state – and it's normal.

One dear friend said to me 'You are so lucky to have loved and been loved – Nobody has ever really loved me like that'. And I know she is right. To grieve is the price we pay for love.

RELIGION

Why would God let this happen? He/she was a good person yet taken before their time. They did all the right things and never hurt anybody. I've asked that question and I don't even believe in God. For those with a strong religious belief maybe there is a degree of comfort in thinking that they will meet again with their loved one in some sort of after-life. Sadly I do not have that belief and it would be hypocritical to try to engender it. Each to their own.

I actually envy those who believe – even if they have no-one left to live for they will have someone to die for! If I truly believed I'd be reunited with my husband in heaven I'd swallow the entire contents of the medicine cupboard in order to be with him again. To love someone deeply is a cruel virtue when that person is snatched away. And yes, again I say – it's normal to feel anger and rage against whatever deity you worship. It's not fair – nothing in life is.

JUST ONE MORE TIME

Walk with me bare-foot in the sand
See clear our imprints – firm and strong
In rippling waves along the shore
Soon, in an instance, washed and gone

Like dreams we cherished dashed away
Happiness torn from our fragile clasp
Our future stolen – no bright horizon
Love and laughter a memory past

Feel the sunshine now before clouds gather
To blight our day and break our hearts
Today, my love, we'll walk together
Cast off the dread that soon we'll part

Hold my hand in the lapping waves
Just one more time – forget our fears
Let's reminisce our happy past
Today we'll smile and dry our tears

COPING

Coping ... what's that? You don't 'cope'. Getting out of bed ... getting into bed ... that is struggle enough. Being bothered to wash – what's the point? My hair was a stringy mess for weeks. It doesn't matter ... it's normal. Existing in an old dressing gown (his) and hiding your tear-stained swollen face from the world ... that's grief. Coping in the aftermath of death is a whole new ball-game where there are no rules and no instruction book!

For now friends and family 'cope' for you, care for you, get you through the tsunami of shock. They will sit quietly beside you while every tune on the radio grates. The television stays switched off as you will scream at the puerile rubbish spouting from the mouths of presenters.

It's difficult for those not yet touched by deep grief to appreciate the abnormity of your feelings ... the weakness; the inability to tackle the smallest task. Stress that makes you unable even to think of how to make a cup of tea.

This is when loving family and friends are needed – let them help. My daughters did all the paperwork – which was (and still is) mountainous. My sons-in-law sorted the car, garden and garage. My grandsons cleared some of my husband's hobby things and cut the grass. My granddaughter sorted out my 'phone. All this kindness ... how I love them all.

My friends ... seeing me torn apart, rescued me so many times. When my kitchen floor flooded at seven in the morning, they were there with a spanner under the sink. When my cooker and hob refused to come on, they were there with a multimeter (whatever that is). When the valve stuck on the fish-pond filter, when the gutter blocked up with leaves, when the integral bed-side light refused to come on and when my printer decided to die an untimely death ... they were there. Maybe they didn't really understand why a normally competent woman could no longer cope with these mundane household problems ... but they came anyway. Such is true friendship.

This chapter seems to be about me and my experience, but as I know this is how you will be feeling too, I make no apology. Let yourself be helped. Practical as well as emotional assistance can be life-saving and reduce the stress you are facing every day. A man with a plunger when the sink blocks up is worth his weight in gold.

Your friends want to help. Sometimes they don't know how. Practical help is something they are able to give. Emotional help is much more difficult. Men in particular are at a total loss coping with the wailing banshee that I've become – they would far rather come round with a couple of rawl plugs and a hammer to help out in a practical way. Yes, I will be forever grateful. Perhaps when I am stronger I will be able to help them if they are ever thrown into the melting pot of turmoil caused by grief.

You are Gone

Yet Still the Roses Bloom

THE DREADED POST

I actually welcome junk mail now as I can simply chuck it in the re-cycling bin. Have you ever seen a speeded-up version of the rear car lights on a motorway? Streaks of angry red all merged into one fragmented blur. That is the mind of the bereaved. To sort through post and make sense of it all is impossible. Months on I still try to do little jobs just to put off opening the post. Anything to delay the moment of unfolding the letters which you know will present more problems.

The brown ones are just awful – HMRC – Her Majesty's Revenue & Customs. I can't believe Her Majesty really hates me so much as to sanction these inexplicable demands that the Tax Office send out in her name. I don't read them any more – let them do their worst. I really don't care if my tax is right or wrong. And Probate – the endless questions and months of sorting out. Bills, insurance, pensions, it just goes on and on. The exhaustion of your grief is so much more demanding – let it all wait. If a kind friend or relative can help – it's good to let them. The burden of trying to deal with paperwork is totally overwhelming.

And 'The Bank'. Half a tree of paper drops through the letter-box every other day. Inheritance, ISA's, Savings, Accounts, Direct Debits – keep them open, close them down. Being newly bereaved it's a minefield of muddle and sadly, for most of us, it still is a few months down the line.

This book is to share the despondency of our grief and not to give advice. But, I would say one thing: Don't be in a rush to change anything, especially if it involves money. Our minds are in no fit state to make logical judgements and we could easily be swayed by the opinions of others. If you're unsure, wait a while. Let time help clarify your thoughts – however long it takes.

We all need an outlet for the anger in our grief. A very satisfying way to release this pent-up rage is to scream down the phone at the scammer who wants to 'mend' your computer, or the fraudster who tells you your credit card has been cloned! Call him/her all the names under the sun – they are not likely to report you, are they?

I still yell hysterically at the companies who demand to 'speak' to my husband three months after he died even though I've told them. One company, who should know better as they specifically deal with the over 50's, received an email from me that should have exploded their computer when they sent my husband an insurance renewal document after they had been informed of his death. Do you know what their excuse was? (and they're not the only firm to make this excuse) – It's the computer!!! The computer, my eye. Computers operate on the information put in by human beings – or in the case of some companies – dopey idiots!

HER MAJESTY'S REVENUE & CUSTOMS (HMRC)

In the name of Her Majesty
Elizabeth, our Queen
Those at the Inland Revenue
Send rules I mustn't contravene

I've tax codes by the dozen
Directives by the score
My letter-box has buckled
And they've wrecked the parquet floor

I think the Inland Revenue
Cut down an extra tree
To turn it into paper
And post it all to me

I've come to the conclusion
That Her Majesty, for sure
Must hold a grudge against me
To send such missives to my door

I'm complaining to Her Majesty
Take their bitter pill and suck it
I bet they don't put her through this
When Philip kicks the bucket

So I'll return them to the Palace
Addressing them: Dear Queen
They've sent these to me in your name
You can have them back, Love Jean

Her
Majesty's
Revenue and
Customs

When I started this poem, I was in a mood of utter frustration, bombarded with official letters, each bringing more problems. It really wasn't meant to be funny – sarcastic perhaps! But if you have found it amusing, then I hope I've made you smile – it is allowed!

MADNESS

Anyone reading this book who is not bereaved will think it the disjointed ramblings of a mad woman – and they're probably right. The first madness is the madness of grief, the second is the madness of anger, and they merge. Friends will suggest we talk to our missing loved one … fine … but when there's no reply, the silence is overwhelming. So, the madness of grief we display talking to an empty chair, and the madness of anger when he doesn't answer, when we feel we could slap the silly, so much loved, grin off his face in the photo. Anger that he's left us to grieve without his support.

And the third madness – the madness of insanity … yes, we can feel it knocking on our door and it frightens us. If we open that door the floodgates will burst. Such is our fear, the tight grip that we exercise to gain control makes our body go rigid and our mind a highway of buzzing wires. What can we do? Open a bottle of wine, eat chocolate … No, that's what we do on a bad hair day.

I wish I could tell you what to do but I can't … not yet anyway. I grip the edges of the chair and hold on until the intensity passes and the dull ache returns. Such is the madness we share. You are not alone in this feeling … it's normal … it's grief. Only you and I, and others who have loved deeply and lost, share this emotion and will understand. The enormity of feeling is too great to comprehend if you haven't experienced it.

For the Beauty of a Rose
There's the Pain of a Thorn

ADJUSTMENT

As months go by we'll experience guilt ... yes ... guilt. It's crazy. We should be 'getting over it', 'moving on', 'dried the tears' ... and we feel guilty that we don't feel that way yet. So we pretend that we're getting better so that we don't upset anybody. When a well-meaning person asked if I was OK now I actually heard myself say 'I'm fine' when I really wanted to shriek 'How the bloody hell do you think I'm feeling'. 'Fine' ... who am I kidding – not myself, but they seemed happier on hearing my glib and totally untrue response. It lets them off the emotional hook somehow. In consideration of other people's feelings after all these months, I put on an act. Pretty convincing – the only person I don't fool is myself. Such is the actress within me.

And yet, perhaps I have made some sort of progress from the lethargy I felt in the early days. Today I screwed the knob back on the cupboard door ... I actually found a Phillips screwdriver and did it. Yes ... thinking about it ... from being incapable of cutting my own toenails a few months ago, that is a real leap in my so called 'recovery'.

What am I really trying to share with you in this chapter? People, friends, relatives have a stereotype expectation of us to 'move on'... how I hate that phrase! They cannot sustain the level of emotional and practical support they so willingly gave in the early days. They can't 'phone us every morning for the rest of their lives just to make sure we have woken up and not swallowed the entire contents of the medicine cupboard in an effort to ensure oblivion.

Some 'friends', those same people who promised us unending support until their dying day, ease off and contact us less and less. We are an odd number at their 'couples' dinner parties. Let them go. Our life-style has changed; we're no longer half of a couple. The true and loyal friends who stay by us, and the new, mostly single friends we will make are all worth ten of those who have drifted out of our lives. They are our future.

As one wise widow said to me: You make many adjustments in your life; when you marry, when you have children, when you retire, and the worst of all, the adjustment you make when you lose a partner. I think this is the hardest because it's not an adjustment you share and tackle together. However good family and friends are, you face it alone. The other adjustments are all made by choice; no-one chooses the adjustment caused by bereavement. We have joined the club nobody wants to join!

YESTERDAY I WAS HAPPY

The big 'C'
Who can say the word
It creeps up oh so stealthily
Silent and unheard

Tendrils of evil torment
The cancer – will it spread
Yesterday I was happy
Tomorrow's full of dread

BE KIND TO YOURSELF

Treat yourself kindly. Just for a while think only of yourself. Do exactly what you feel like doing. If you want to follow the jelly-babies and marshmallows diet – go for it. If you chose to eat four Mars bars for lunch and three packs of Haribos for dinner, that's fine. This was my eating pattern in the immediate aftermath of my husband's death. You will go through these stages. In the short term it really doesn't matter.

I also eat a lot of bread and jam, bread and Marmite, bread and peanut-butter, bread and chocolate spread. Sensible friends will advise you to cook some nourishing meals for yourselves. They're right, of course, but it just doesn't seem worth the effort. If you've eaten a healthy diet in the past you'll probably revert back to it sometime in the future – when the future actually begins to matter to you again. At the moment it's all too much of an effort.

If, like me, you just want to curl up in your dressing-gown clutching a hot-water-bottle and deny the rest of the world exists, then do just that. Whatever helps you get through the first few weeks.

This book isn't about giving advice; it's about the sharing and understanding of pain. It's about surviving the unhappiest time of our lives. I did endeavour to 'pull myself together' and it wouldn't be right if I didn't urge you also to try to take little steps towards digging yourselves out of the quagmire of heartache that you find yourself in.

A lady who had been widowed for many years said that I must try to accept all the invitations issued to me. To join in all the events I could possibly face in the company of others. This advice I do try to take – but it's hard. Being in the company of others enjoying a meal or whatever, is a real strain and sometimes it all ends in tears. We must try but to be in the midst of a social gathering is the loneliest time of all. How can their world go on when yours and mine have stopped? How can the music still play?

Many friends invited me for meals – they must have formed a rota to keep me fed and this did help – it kept my strength up as I really didn't bother to eat – I don't bother much now if I'm truthful, even after all these months.

For each step forward towards some sort of normality sometimes it seems we take two steps backwards. There is no normality. Nothing will ever be normal again. But we must try, if only for the sake of those around us. But be kind to yourself.

MAKE BARGAINS WITH YOURSELF

Talk to yourself and make bargains. Say to yourself, 'When the clock says 9.00 I'll get up and put my dressing-gown on'. 'When it says 9.15 I'll make a cup of coffee'; 'at 9.30 I'll have a shower'; 'at 9.45 I'll get dressed'. Just tiny steps to progress through the long day ahead with some semblance of order. Just for a little while you'll feel in control.

For someone like me, who was always leaping out of bed at 6.00 anticipating another happy day with my lovely husband, family and friends, this is a major adjustment and it will be for you too – I truly understand. The change in routine is huge. No-one to make you a cup of tea in bed; no-one to listen to the news on the radio with; no-one to share opinions on events both big and small happening in the world. Only you. Only you can see the first rose of summer in the garden or the family of bluetits visiting the bird-table – and it's so lonely – I know.

Say to yourself, 'Today I'll wash my hair before I eat that chunk of cake which I'm going to call lunch'. Add another little 'bargain' each day – just to get you through the long and lonely hours; to still the panic you feel and maintain a level of calm. 'At 10.00 I'll vacuum the carpet for just five minutes' – this is a big step forward as in the beginning you would not have known how to switch the Hoover on much less had the energy to push it around.

I actually know what seven of the buttons on my remote control are for now. Out of forty-six buttons, I still have a long way to go, but seven is an achievement – don't knock it. What the other thirty-nine buttons do is a complete mystery, but it doesn't matter. If you are now able to switch on the T.V. and watch a programme – and even better – if you can follow what is being said – you have indeed made a fundamental step forward on the road called 'bereavement'.

The first time you spontaneously laugh, or feel joy again, is probably a long way off – if ever I hear you say and I understand – I too am waiting for that moment. But to take back control of your life in little ways helps. To go to the shops; to actually think what you need instead of looking at the packed shelves in total bewilderment is progress.

But don't hold the reins of control too tightly – sometime you just need to curl up and cry. And it's normal.

A REASON TO GET UP

Getting out of bed – the hardest part of the day. To feel that wave of depression and pointless negativity. Once again as we surface from sleep we feel that brick still lodged in our chest and our throat is tight. Yes, it's normal. I sleep – thanks to the 'magic' pills – but I know and share how you feel. All mornings are bad, some are just awful. How many more months, years, before we wake up in happy anticipation of the day ahead? The first tears of the day seep into our pillow.

You probably, like me, still sleep in a double bed. You may be physically warm under the duvet on 'your' side, but we reach out and 'his' side of the bed is cold. You may, again like me, wrap your arms round his pillow, but his 'scent' has faded and offers little comfort now. Only the bereaved can feel this depth of hollow emptiness and there are so many of us. This level of grief is never talked about. Too embarrassing for the listener. The whole point of my writing this book is to explore and share this depth of emotion with you. To make you feel less alone and, I hope, provide a vestige of comfort.

Before you go to bed try to think of a reason to get up the next morning. Try to wake with that thought in your head. Last night I de-frosted some stewing-steak (I am trying to eat properly – occasionally!). It needs an onion with it. My reason to get out of bed today is to buy that onion. So, I have to get up, wash, get dressed, go out, drive the car, find the onions in the supermarket and pay the bill. All huge achievements on the path of bereavement when you can't work out what day of the week it is sometimes. And all because I need an onion. An onion's not worth showering for – I'll do that tomorrow when I have to get up and go to SpecSavers!

Those in your life who have not yet lost a person they loved deeply will read this as total gibberish. But you and I know it's true and will identify with every word. So, before you try to sleep tonight give yourself a reason to wake up. Something you want to do, or need to do, it doesn't matter. Hold it in your mind and cling on to it. Even if it is just to buy an onion!

ALONE

In the morning and in the evening there is only you. Only you to see the tears you shed first thing as you face another day. Only you to see the sunrise. It may be months or even years since that one special person in our life died but the loneliness is palpable. That sick empty feeling in our stomach, the negative thoughts, the stress of coping with everything life hurls at us now we're alone. Although we may have supportive friends and a caring family, at the end of the day we feel so vulnerable and it's normal – we're grieving.

I have tried to be my own comforter and best friend. There are many who choose to live very successful lives alone, but if we've been part of a loving couple for half a century (sixty years in my case) living alone is quite alien and we're lost. Completely unable to establish any sort of routine now that the old life-style has been so cruelly obliterated – we are only half a person.

But, of course, we must try. Try to do something positive each day. Today I'm going to try to change the ink cartridge in the printer (always one of his jobs in the past). I don't know how to do it and can feel waves of panic caused by the stress of even thinking about it. But I must try. Those who haven't suffered the stress of loss will struggle to understand this ... believe me, it's normal. Taking on his role, all the little jobs he did without even thinking about them, is monumental.

Make a decision not to think ... don't think ... don't think ... don't think ... just DO! Make a list of just little positive things: dust the mirror in the hall; buy some bananas; vacuum the study; make an appointment with the dentist. I know – we don't care if all our teeth fall out ... but try. By just ticking off three or four little things can be a step towards being in control.

Gradually, just for a few minutes, we'll feel we've achieved something. It's a start. Add a little positive step to that list each day. Little steps, little challenges, little ticks as each is achieved. I know we won't ever reach the end of the lonely road we are walking, and we will take major steps backwards, but perhaps one day a weak glimmer of light will shine through the end of the very dark tunnel we find ourselves in. Don't think ... don't think ... don't think ... take my hand, deep breath ... calm ... calm ... don't think ... just get out of the chair and try to do it.

Good advice I was given: If you can't do something the first time, stop; have a glass of wine or a cup of tea and then try again. If you still can't do it ask for help. We'll probably drink lots of wine or cups of tea but let's give that a try together.

Postscript to this chapter: I did it! I changed the printer ink cartridge. I stopped, nearly gave up, had that cup of tea, and tried again – success! My fingers may be covered in ink but for one nanosecond I felt a sense of triumph. Sad really, but the bereaved will understand.

Only Love Remains

AUTUMN LOVE

Autumn love is special
Not like that of fickle Spring
Or restless with a molten heat
That Summer love can bring

Autumn love is gentle
As the dove rests after flight
A pearly dawn and drifting mist
The moonbeams of the night

Autumn love is peaceful
No more the thunderous roar
As sparkling waves caress the sand
And lap the golden shore

Autumn love is comfort
A hand to hold, a heart to care
Mellowed with fulfilment
To cherish and to share

Autumn love is tranquil
As a rainbow's fading hue
And this season of our love
Is the gift I give to you

THE HUG OF A STRANGER

As time passes and the rawness blunts we erect a shield around ourselves so that nothing can penetrate and hurt us. We avoid events and places that bring back painful memories. But no shield is impenetrable. Flashbacks happen unexpectedly and leave us exposed.

Today I re-lived the terrible time of the month before my husband died when each day I would catch the bus to be with him in hospital. This morning I had to take the same bus for an appointment of my own. As I got on the bus the floodgates opened – I felt I was visiting my husband again and he would be waiting for me – our eyes would lock as I walked into the little ward he was in. Raw emotion is uncontrollable and I cried. Tears rained down my face on that Number 4 bus. A friend actually got on the same bus further along the route and sat with me and held my hand while I tearfully tried to explain why I was crying.

Once in the hospital I had to walk through the well-remembered corridors and pass the ward where he died and I had another unnerving flashback. It was seven in the morning – a Sunday. I was spending all my time at the hospital to be with my dear husband in his final days. I was walking along a dim deserted corridor and a lady was walking a few steps ahead of me. Our footsteps echoed. Just the two of us in that eerie empty corridor. I drew abreast and we turned to look at each other. We were both crying. The stranger and I stood together for a moment sadly shaking our heads. Then spontaneously we hugged each other – for what seemed like a long time we clung together – this stranger and I. Then we gave each other a sad tearful little smile – no words were spoken. She turned into the Acute Stroke Ward and I headed on to the Cancer Ward.

I will never forget that stranger. We shared such compassion. The hug of a stranger brought immeasurable comfort and just for those few minutes we were united in our grief. Oh, how I would like to meet that lovely lady again. We shared a poignant moment in our lives which we will never forget.

Is there a way to avoid flashbacks? No, I don't think so. We try not to expose ourselves to painful memories but sometimes they are unavoidable. The chair our loved one sat in will always remain empty.

The best we can do is make changes, do different things, concentrate on activities that he wasn't involved with. Don't go down memory lane until we are ready – it's too painful. Perhaps, in time, we will be able to look back with a smile but at the moment favourite 'together' places are best avoided – why do anything that intensifies our grief. Let's be kind to ourselves and keep the shield up.

MEMORIES

How often I have heard the phrase 'You have all your wonderful memories'. Yes, and they are wonderful, but it's difficult to live on memories when we know those happy, picture post-card times, are now out of our reach. It makes our loss even deeper somehow. We may make different memories in the years to come but 'wonderful'? – it's hard to imagine. Sometimes thinking about them just rubs salt into an open wound.

One of my wonderful memories is dancing with my husband on the deck of a cruise ship in the moonlight as we crossed the equator. Him in a dress suit and me in a long sparkling midnight blue dress. I can still see the velvet star-studded sky and hear the gentle swish of the ocean. We danced alone – the music drifting up from the ballroom on the deck below. And it was magical. I remember it so well – but now that memory brings sadness as I know it can never happen again. We can no longer dance together.

The time we trekked in the Amazon jungle; the helicopter trip over New York; the holiday when we saw the magnificent Iguazu Falls in Brazil and Argentina. All those memories and many more, but all tinged with sadness because whatever we do in the future will be without the one we love the most and want to be with. Memories are bitter-sweet.

You and I will remember events such as these as 'the big ones', but every-day life is not really made up of spectacular memories, they are one offs. Nobody crosses the equator or treks in the jungle every day of the week. It's the mundane memories that hurt the most. The daily reminders of our loss. Nobody to wrap my pyjamas around a hot-water-bottle so they are nice and warm when I get into bed. Nobody to make me a cup of tea when I'm cold and tired. No-one to de-frost the car on an icy morning. No-one to cook a nice meal for; no shirts to iron or socks to darn. No-one to kiss goodnight. I know that in my old-fashioned happy marriage I was a very lucky and pampered wife. Never having lived alone makes it all the harder to cope now.

And no-one to nag anymore! How I miss seeing the magazines scattered on the floor around his chair that I would have to pick up. Or his coat slung over the bannister instead of being hung on a hanger. Oh, I would so love to be able to nag again!

I have related much of my own experience in this section. You will have your own bitter-sweet memories. Hold them tightly to you – perhaps one day we'll be able to smile as we think back. Until then remember we loved and were loved. And now we pay the price with our grieving.

COMPANY

Sometimes when we feel down and particularly unhappy we don't want the company and chatter of everybody around us. At these times don't dismiss the loving sympathy and quiet comfort so freely and generously given by animals.

Both my daughters have dogs and they 'lend' them to me. Jakey is a beautiful large black Labrador and Jasmine the cutest and mischievous little Yorkie. When tears well up in my eyes Jakey will immediately get as much of himself as he can on my lap and nuzzle his big soft head on my shoulder. I rest my cheek against his face – his eyes speak words that no-one could think to say and his understanding is total. Jasmine continues to search the house for Grandad – he was one of her favourite people. She will wait by the door watching for him and sit by his chair. We share a longing for the past and we will cuddle up under the duvet together. The physical warmth of their bodies, the sadness, love and care in their eyes is beyond belief. Never under-estimate animals.

We can all benefit from non-human company. Who can fail to be cheered by the robins squabbling for seed on the bird-table, or the joy of seeing a rare nuthatch or a jay in the garden. Each morning when I feed the fish in my pond, Trouty, a huge ghost carp, will take food from my hand, and I watch them endlessly.

And my handsome wild fox who visits me each evening and, bathed in the radiance of the security light, sits on my patio and looks at me through the conservatory window. I know he only comes for the scraps I put out for him, but he is an enormous comfort during the long lonely evenings and I wait for him to appear. If I have no scraps I make him a cheese sandwich! I've assumed it is a 'him'. How lucky I would be if it was a vixen – she could one day bring her cubs to visit of an evening – that would be a delight.

I don't have dogs or cats of my own for two reasons. One is that they tie you down – I couldn't spend the day out walking if I had a dog dependent on me at home; and secondly, they are an expense – insurance, vets bills, food etc. This has to be considered, but if you can afford to have a pet, and circumstances permit, think about it. The warmth and comfort given by a loving and well-loved animal cannot be measured in words.

YOUR EMPTY CHAIR

It's so long since I've seen you
Please sit in your chair once more
Let me hear the sound of your laughter
The turn of your key in the door

Let me see you with flowers in the garden
Sit beside me when driving the car
In my dreams I still hold you to me
When awake your distance is far

With your voice the room will still echo
Your photo smiles out from its frame
The love-letters tied with blue ribbon
Each one precious and bearing your name

Take your place at the dining-room table
Together a dinner we'll share
Please come back so we'll be together
Just once more, please sit in your chair

FEAR

When talking with other widows I've been amazed by the feelings we share with each other that we don't share with the outside world. We don't talk about things that frighten or worry us because those who have never lost a close and loving partner will probably not understand and think us stupid – even laugh at our fears.

An outwardly competent lady who has been a widow for over two years explained that she is terrified – each morning she wakes up panic-stricken and frightened – we agreed it was illogical, but that fear truly exists. And what are we afraid of? Things going wrong that we can't control and can't fix and have no-one to share our magnified worries with.

Please God – don't let the computer crash today, please don't let the car break down, or the washing machine flood the kitchen, or the television go wrong. Don't let the taps leak or the toilet block up – because I don't know what to do.

The enormity of tackling these problems even some years following bereavement is so real, yet our fears are concealed and held within ourselves. I identified with her words as each day I feel a sense of trepidation that life will hurl something else at me. Worries are intensified out of proportion in the early sleepless hours when we're alone. I recognise that it's silly but we can't control that fear. Perhaps our reaction is brought about by a sense of insecurity and vulnerability, we're only half a person now and we are on our own. We don't have the confidence to tackle all the problems we didn't think twice about in the past. We feel that if just one more thing goes wrong we'll crack.

For many of us there is the added fear of managing our finances. No so bad if funds are adequate to cover all the extra expenditure needed when we cope alone, but for those of us who struggle to make ends meet, this is another challenge – everything that goes wrong costs money. Cutting back the high hedge, cleaning the gutters, all the little jobs that he did are beyond us now and have to be paid for. As the saying goes 'Life's a bitch and then you die!' Yes, true, but in our case part of us has already died.

I'm sure we widows are on a 'suckers' list somewhere. We must be on our guard against being taken advantage of. I had a scruffy looking yob standing on my doorstep saying he'd 'Tarmac my drive for fifty quid, love'. Seeing as I have a block-paving drive he must have thought I was totally stupid. I quickly shut the door but it was unnerving. The old me would have faced him squarely and told him to 'bugger off'. I'm no longer that person!

My energy supplier decided that I had used God knows how many millions of units of electricity and wanted to charge me £1,750 pounds for just over six weeks supply. Totally impossible and obviously wrong. But ... and this is what scared me ... they said they were sending a bill for this amount. I spoke to a couple of other widows and they said they too would have absolutely freaked out! My two sensible daughters laughed and said that it was just a mistake and could be put right which, after five phone calls, each with a rising level of desperation, it was. But the fact is, while my rational daughters simply dismissed the issue, I lay awake each night imagining bailiffs banging on the front door as my fertile brain calculated that I would owe them over £15,000 by the end of the year if it carried on at this rate. How would I face the neighbours if that happened ... see how the mind of the bereaved slips so easily into over-drive!

We are weakened by our loss. For now we are unable to 'hold our own' easily. We keep our thoughts to ourselves and could easily be bullied into entering an agreement which we would normally view with suspicion. So – let's try – even though we are widowed – our views matter. You are still a person – you still have rights – you still have opinions – you are still important. Even though we feel our brain power has been reduced to the level of a processed pea, let's try to voice our thoughts and feelings. You will be surprised at the support you'll receive from all the brave souls struggling alone.

Postscript: This is a chapter to which I must add a postscript – to give encouragement for the future. The learning curve for those of us of a certain age left behind in this lunatic world of unfathomable technology is immense, but today I clawed my way through the jungle and had a Smart Meter fitted for gas and electricity, the work taking place in the deep mid-winter. When the very nice young fitter left I had to deal with all the electrical appliances that were flashing and bleeping at me – and I did!

Well, mostly! I have no central heating on the upstairs landing, shower room or back bedrooms – we couldn't afford to have it installed when the extension was built – so I have individual heaters on timers. The fact that the shower room electric radiator will probably come on for just thirty minutes at three in the morning and the room will be icy when I get up, the landing heater will rebel and do its own thing, and I won't have any hot water is very likely. I haven't quite got the hang of setting timers yet, but the fact that I have now, after all these months, regained the confidence to try is all that matters. I'll get it right in the end – and so will you.

Meanwhile I owe another huge thank-you to those lovely friends who appear with a spanner in one hand and an oily rag in the other to dig me out of trouble. What would I do without them!

SHOPPING FOR ONE

Months down the line we must try shopping for one – a healthy shop – not just bits and pieces. I actually bought a head of broccoli and, if you're like me, you won't have had anything green in your fridge for a long time (apart from the odd spot of mould which, in the scheme of things, really doesn't seem to matter much). We will never have shopped for one before – it's a whole new experience – we shopped for the family or as a couple, but this is new ... this is painful. There's too much of everything. Our minds quickly cloud with confusion and we remember the times we shopped together – probably with him pushing the trolley and sneaking in a few extra goodies or moaning about how long we were taking just looking at everything. So we're off to a shaky start.

But one good thing came out of today's venture ... I felt anger – pure rage – and that's so much better than the feeling of fragile vulnerability we have lived with for so long. Anger gave me empowerment. For just a moment the fragility of a gossamer wing was replaced by the seething resentment of a bull elephant!

What caused it? I'll tell you! I wanted yogurt. I could have two six-packs for £3.00 (£1.50 each) or one pack for £2.00. I can't eat twelve yogurts so would have to pay the extra unit price. That's so unfair.

OK – forget the yogurt. Runner-beans next. Again, two packs were £2.00 or one pack £1.50. This is pure exploitation and hits the elderly, widowed and single people very hard below the belt and in the pocket.

What did I do? Well, I made a complete exhibition of myself. I shouted at the poor lad sorting the bananas – probably a sixth-former earning extra pocket money on a Saturday morning. I was quite at my explosive best when approached by the supervisor, then collapsed in floods of tears, and headed for the jelly-babies. It was not a success.

Postscript to this chapter. I posted this on social media via my Facebook page. I was amazed at the support for my rant. It seems I am not alone in feeling this is unfair. I've never really recognised this exploitation before but it is practised in most supermarkets. We widows should band together and boycott any items that promote this marketing method. Life's hard enough without rubbing our noses in it!

BE SAFE

Some clot, with the sensitivity of a brick, asked me if I thought I would ever marry again. For me – NO! Definitely not. I'm only interested in men if they come with a spanner in one hand and an oily rag in the other to sort out something that is blocked, jammed, broken or bleeping at me.

On the other hand, I can understand those who seek the comfort of another person to share their lives. Loneliness is soul destroying and to try to create another happy union, to relive the good times, is understandable. I've known widows marry again in haste but, sadly, repent at leisure. One person cannot be replaced by another.

And if you're a wealthy widow, be particularly wary. There are a lot of unscrupulous rogues out there. If you're eighty-two and he's twenty-eight, it's not your body he's after, it's your bank account. Keep the guard up. As they say; 'If it's too good to be true, it probably is'. There's many a wolf in sheep's clothing. Be suspicious and keep yourself safe.

STAY WITH ME

If you come to me in dreams
Then I will welcome sleep
If you're with me in the shadows
Then my grief won't be so deep

Sing to me a song that soothes
Ease the breaking of my heart
Speak to me of things we loved
Help me through now we're apart

Sit beside me in the garden
Stroll woodlands as we walk
In memory we're together
As in silence we still talk

Now I go on without you
And empty is your chair
In spirit we're together
In my heart you're always there

HO, HO, HO AND JINGLE BELLS

How do we cope with them? Anniversaries, Christmas and New Year, Birthdays – all the happy times that used to bring such joy. For some minor events the actress within me will rise to the surface and I cope. But it's not easy, is it? Our faces may be rigid, our throats so tight we can't speak – even after months of being alone the hurt is still acute, and we must try to smile – it's expected of us. The first Christmas, carols around the tree sparkling with tinsel, turkey with all the trimmings, mulled wine and mistletoe, and all without the one we have stood beside and loved and shared our lives with. The enhancement of our sad situation is devastating – and even if we hang on tight to our rein of control at some point we will weaken.

And those Christmas cards! If you can't face just writing from 'me' when you've always written from 'him and me' – then don't send any. Explain to your friends and family and wish them a happy Christmas on the internet. Perhaps many won't understand – let them think you're safe-guarding the environment and cutting down on paper! It doesn't matter what they think – really, it doesn't.

Some Christmas cards we receive will obviously have been chosen with great care and compassion – they will simply say something like 'Thinking of You'. It is a comfort to know that people have actually chosen a card especially for us and in recognition of our hurt and despair at this time. It may be the season to be merry for most but for the newly bereaved our acute sense of loss will be paramount.

One card I received, sent by somebody with the sensitivity of a short plank, said 'Merry Christmas and Have a Great New Year'. This message just blurred with tears. I'm sure some people don't even think about the words on cards; they don't mean to make things worse and we must try not to cry at all the 'Merry' Christmas messages – but it hurts so much. If you're supporting somebody who has lost a loved one, think about how they will be coping and please read the message on the card before you post it – the last thing that they feel is 'merry'. The newly bereaved spend much of their life alone with their thoughts and have time to actually read all the words on the cards.

We must not feel 'obliged' to go Christmas shopping – all the glitz and glitter, the music, the lights, the bustle, the noise, don't help the way we feel. We are on the side – almost an on-looker regarding the pantomime of happiness all around that we are no longer part of. Our minds are still in turmoil and trying to decide what to get everybody is just too stressful. I made the decision to get vouchers – perhaps I took the cowards' way out but we must be kind to ourselves if we are to survive the festive season in one piece.

As one wise widow said – 'It does get easier in time'. Does it? If, like me, the jury's still out on that one, don't feel bad – it's normal – you're not alone. Perhaps things will get easier in time, but there are no short-cuts on the road of bereavement – each of us making that journey will take however long it takes.

It would hurt if our friends and family didn't ask us to join them but, especially if the celebration is with couples – our old comfortable 'couples' set of friends – we end up wishing we hadn't gone – we could have spared ourselves the pain. And New Year's Eve, when on the stroke of midnight all the couples will turn to each other and kiss, the loneliness we feel is heart-breaking.

How do we smile and sing Auld Lang Syne as if everything in our life is wonderful and we're anticipating another joyful year. We wish to the very depth of our being we could just curl up and die. I know, it's bordering on morbid, but we, the newly bereaved will recognise the truth. The solution, if possible, is to get together with other widows or single folk – a new circle of friends who are in the same boat. At least then we'll be singing from the same hymn sheet.

Advice – I wish I could give solace but you and I know there is nothing which will really help. At two minutes to midnight I will shut myself in the toilet, lock the door and cry. And that's the best advice I can think of realistically giving. Practise self-preservation and put up the shield. Hide from it – just for a little while. Let's spare ourselves the pain of witnessing the happiness of everyone else when we feel so bloody awful! There are so many bereaved souls out there trying to be brave – we're not alone.

We do wish all our friends and family a Happy New Year, of course we do. And it's definitely not jealousy on our part that prevents us joining in the knees-up round the Christmas tree. Envy – the green eye – is what we feel when a friend wears the same dress at the party and she's a perfect size twelve and we're bulging in a size sixteen because we've followed the jelly-babies and marshmallows diet for the past goodness knows how long! No, it's not jealousy. It's the sense of being totally alone in a crowd. We'd be hurt if they left us out but we hurt witnessing life going on around us at the 'Jingle Bells' time when our life remains empty.

And people don't know what presents to buy for the bereaved. One friend bought me a pair of flashing earrings – oh yes – just what I feel like wearing! This is what you would buy somebody to cheer them up after a minor upset. Probably best stick to handkerchiefs or bath sets. But don't be hard on your friends, they struggle too. Each and every one of them would make things better if they could and I am so grateful to them all.

Just at certain times of the year the actress within me crumples!

The first Christmas is not one we look forward to with joyful anticipation

Postscript to this chapter: I've just experienced my first Christmas as a widow – was it easy? – NO! But cushioned within the warmth of a loving and sensitive family I got through it. The actress within me worked hard at times, not wanting to put a damper on the festivities with my tears and spoil Christmas for everyone who had worked so hard to make it bearable for me. There were occasions when I shut myself away and cried and other times when I tried to pretend he was just out of sight in another room.

I was tempted to go back on this chapter and re-write it in a more positive frame of mind, but that wouldn't be right. The words were written when I was in the early and blackest weeks of bereavement and, if you are now at that stage, you will identify with every word and it would be wrong to diminish the intense dread I know you will be feeling – that is normal. By adding this postscript I hope for the future to cast a little light and comfort into the tunnel of darkness in which you currently find yourself enveloped and encourage you to face it.

The very worst part for me was coming back home to a cold, empty, dark, silent house, walking upstairs to the bedroom clutching my little suitcase, and finding a damp patch on the bedroom ceiling. The 'aloneness' swamped me and the floodgates opened and I cried all the tears I had held back over Christmas.

And on 31st January ... at midnight ... that date and time I feared ... some of the ladies I was with who had been widowed for many years, were able to wish each other a Happy New Year. In time, I hope we will be able to do the same and perhaps, by then, I'll be able to wear my flashing earrings – we'll see.

The Light of Love is Eternal

AND FINALLY

When I started to write this book I thought I was doing it solely for the reader, the bereaved, and those supporting the bereaved. Now I realise that it has helped me; if not to accept – I'm not ready yet – but to take the first steps to adapt.

To adapt is not something we want to do – we don't want change of any kind. It frightens us. We're on a roller-coaster; we're hanging on by our finger-tips, and we want to turn the clock back to a time when we were happy. This we can't do. We now face life as a single person. We must be our own best friend and comforter. We may not be happy but we need to seek some level of contentment within ourselves. We must regain our self-esteem. How hard that will be, but we must try, if only for the sake of our families who have suffered alongside us.

However painful it is, we must seek for some kind of acceptance if we are to survive. For the newly bereaved – and, if I'm honest, for the not so newly bereaved, we see our survival as immaterial – we don't care what happens to us. Life, however, continues to pulsate around us and although, for now, we may exist on the periphery, life with all its ups and downs will go on … and we must go on with it.

The sun is always shining
but its rays are shadowed by the clouds in our heart.
May they one day part and heal our sorrow.

The tortuous road called 'Bereavement' has no end.
Reach out, hold my hand, and we'll walk it together.